The Beginner's Guide to GitHub

Thomas Mailund

The Beginner's Guide to GitHub

Table of Contents

Chapter 1

The Beginner's Guide to GitHub

You have heard about git and GitHub and wanted to know what the buzz is about. That is what I am here to tell you. Or, at least, I am here to give you a quick overview of what you can do with git and GitHub. I won't be able, in the space here, to provide you with an exhaustive list of features—in all honesty, I don't know enough myself to be able to claim expertise with these tools. I am only a frequent user, but I can get you started and give you some pointers for where to learn more. That is what this book is for.

I will tell you how to download and install git on your computer, how to set up an account on GitHub, and how to create repositories there. I will teach you how to use branches to work on different features of your project independently and how to use pull-requests to collaborate with others. I will also show you have GitHub supports an entire ecosystem of tools and web services that can assist you in testing your software and in keeping the quality of your code high.

There is much more to using git and GitHub, but after reading this book, you should know enough to be able to use these tools for your everyday projects. The techniques I describe here covers 99% of the interactions you will have with GitHub. After reading this book, you should know enough about git and GitHub to be able to find what you need in GitHub's documentation or by googling.

Chapter 2

Why version control?

If you are reading this, you are probably already motivated to use version control. Or maybe someone told you that you had to, so you don't have a choice. In any case, I will keep this section short.

There are several benefits to using a version control system when you develop software—or indeed for any situation where you create any piece of data or workflow. I use version control systems when I write books and when I write pipelines for data analysis as well as when I develop software. Some of these benefits are obvious, some perhaps less so.

The most obvious benefits of using a version control system are, of course, version control. With a version control system, you can have all previous versions of your source code, analysis pipeline, book text, etc. at your fingertips, so you can go back and see what has changed over time and revert to previous versions if you find that some changes are not to your liking. If you are working alone on a project, this is the essential feature of a version control system, but these systems also give you ways to collaborate on projects in groups.

With the earliest version control system I used, RCS, you could commit changes to the system and revert to previous versions if what you tried to do didn't pan out. You could lock single files to prevent that people made changes, and thus changes that could conflict with your own, but you couldn't work on a system in parallel the files were locked. With git's successor, CVS, this improved immensely. You could now make changes in parallel, even to the same files, and the system would try to merge modified files when you committed to the central source repository. With systems such as git, working in parallel on projects and being able to merge changes made by different people is take to the extreme. Everyone can have their own copy of a repository, make any changes they want, and the system will support you merging changes whenever you want to. The system is as much about collaboration as it is about version control.

With GitHub, the collaboration aspects are enhanced even further. GitHub provides more than just a place for you to have a git repository for your projects, it gives you discussion forums for your projects, for discussing changes you are experimenting with, for addressing bugs and bug fixes, and for planning future roadmaps of your projects.

Speaking of experiments, another feature commonly found in version control systems, and which is supported excellently by git, is branches of your project. Not only can different people work in parallel with each other, but you can also have subprojects for changes that you work on yourself. You can make branches of your project, for example for bug fixes or feature enhancements, try out different things without messing with the central repository, and if things pan out, you can merge these branches into the repository; if they do not, you can throw the branch away. And, of course, you can collaborate with others on these branches as well, so you can experiment together.

Version control systems are an essential part of any software project. GitHub provides a central repository for your projects and excellent communication tools for collaboration. It offers more than just version control and communication, though. Within the GitHub ecosystem, there is also support for various automatic testing and code review processes.

If many people are collaborating on a project, it can be hard to guarantee a consistent code quality. With GitHub and its ecosystem, you can alleviate this by setting up automatic continuous integration tests. Every time you commit changes to the central repository, these checks will run, and you will get a report of how you are doing. You can use this for regular testing, but you can also get reports on how well your tests are covering your code, or how well your code passes various quality checks.

These checks are not part of a version control system but complement it perfectly. You can get a report of the quality of code at each point in the code's history, and when collaborating, you can see, at a glance, the quality of the proposed changes.

Version control and GitHub is more than just a repository of code changes. It is an ecosystem for development and collaboration and well worth getting familiar with if you plan to make a career out of software development.

Chapter 3

Getting started

Before we get to the exciting part where we learn how to create
and work with repositories, we need to have git installed, and
we need to make an account on GitHub. Most communication
through GitHub goes through a web interface and will be
the same for different platforms, but the software you use
to interact with your code repository will vary according to
which platform you work on. I will assume that you either
use the GitHub Desktop GUI, available on Mac and Windows,
or, if you use Linux, that you are familiar with the command
line.

Installing Git

All software changes over time, and it is possible that what I
write here will be obsolete when you read it. If so, you can
always find up-to-date instructions on how to install git at
git-scm.com.

At the time of writing, the best way to install git on a Linux machine is using the package management system for your distribution, e.g. `yum` or `apt-get`. The package you need to install is called `git-all`.

For Windows and Mac, the easiest way to install git is to install GitHub's GUI, GitHub Desktop, which will also let you install the command-line git tools. Unfortunately GitHub Desktop is not available on Linux yet. To install it on Windows or Mac, go to `https://desktop.github.com` and download the tool.

Once you open the tool, you will have the option of setting up a connection to GitHub.

You don't have an account on GitHub yet, but you can click the link to get one (and skip to the next section to see how you set it up). Once you have set up the account, you can type in your username and password.

After that, you can set up the name and email address you want git to use when you commit changes to a repository. Here, you also have the option of installing command line tools. If you only interact with GitHub through the web and the GUI, you don't need them, but you cannot do everything through the GUI, so you probably do want to install them.

After that, you are done. The tool now gives you the option of finding local repositories. If this is the first time you are using git, you won't have any. You are done.

Getting a GitHub account

If you click the link in GitHub Desktop, you are sent to `http://www.github.com`. Here you can sign up by typing

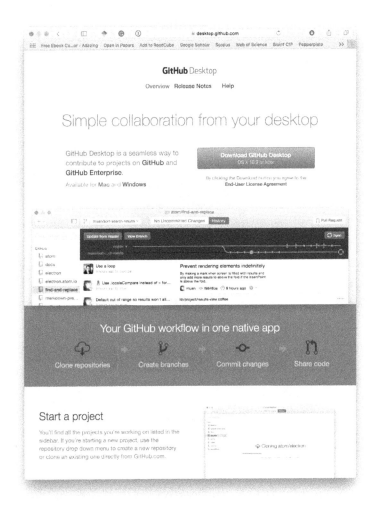

Figure 1: GitHub Desktop download page.

Figure 2: GitHub Desktop welcome screen.

Figure 3: Connect to GitHub screen.

in a username, an email address, and a password. You need to use an email address you have access to since you will be asked to validate it later.

Once you sign up, you get to set up your account plan. You can choose the free plan. The free plan lets you have as many repositories you want, and you have full access to all the features of GitHub. Previously your repositories had to be public if you used the free plan (the screenshot shows the signup page then). Since then, GitHub has also allowed an

Figure 4: Configuer Git screen.

unlimited number of private repositories. A public repository means that others can see your code. If you want to keep your software hidden, you need to use a private repository.

After that, you can provide a little information about yourself. I am not sure if this is used for anything besides informing GitHub of their user base, but just in case you might as well answer honestly here.

Now you are mostly done. You get sent to a page where you can choose between reading the documentation or starting a new project. The latter means setting up a new repository, and we cover that in the next section. If you choose to read

Figure 5: Setup local repositories screen.

Figure 6: Create GitHub account.

the guide, you will get a tutorial that covers virtually the same as I include in this book. I suggest you read both the tutorial and the book—it is often helpful to read the same information more than once if it is written in different ways.

If you choose to start a new project—and eventually you should—you will have to verify your email address. You will be sent an email, and you should click on the link in that email.

Then you can go and set up your profile on GitHub. You can provide as much or as little information as you like here.

Figure 7: Choose a subscription plan.

Setting up a repository

After you have verified your email address, clicking on the Start a project button sends you to a page where you can set up a new repository.

Here you need to give the repository a name—we could create a test repository and call it `hello-world`—and you need to provide it with a short description. It doesn't matter what you give as the description. You can choose whether the repository should be public of private. You can then choose to generate a README file or not. You always want to make a README file. The README file is used to describe your

15

Figure 8: Tell GitHub about yourself.

project and will be displayed on the front web page for your project. You can also choose whether you want to make a .gitignore file and a license. The .gitignore file is used to tell git that specific files should be ignored—you could probably guess that from the name—and you can always add one later. When setting up a repository, generating a .gitignore file is useful if you know which programming language your project will be written in. Different languages create different types of temporary files, and the initial .gitignore file can be set up to ignore those. For our test repository, we don't need a .gitignore file. We don't need a licence file either. Just click Create repository

Figure 9: Take GitHub's tutorial.

Once you have created the repository, you are sent to the central repository page. It is through this page you will do most of your interaction with GitHub. Right now, it just shows you the structure of the code—it is a single file, README.md. The README file is also displayed below the code.

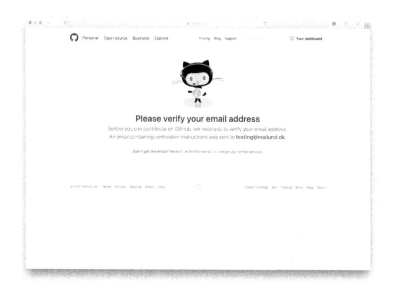

Figure 10: Verify your email.

Figure 11: Your GitHub profile.

Figure 12: Creating a repository.

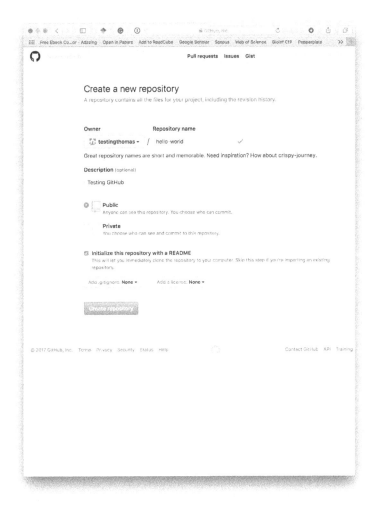

Figure 13: Configuring your repository.

Figure 14: Repository homepage.

Chapter 4

Working with repositories

Once you have created a repository, you need to download it to your own computer. As long as it is just sitting on GitHub it is of no use to you; you need to get hold of it so you can add and modify files.

Cloning repositories

To download the repository, you should click the green Clone or download button on the front page of the repository webpage.

When you click the button, you get a URL for the repository and a choice between Open in Desktop and Download ZIP. We do want to download the repository, but not as a ZIP file. If we download it that way, we get a copy of the current version of the repository, but it will not be set up as a git repository. It will merely be a copy. We want to clone the repository, which means that we get a copy of the full repository—history of all

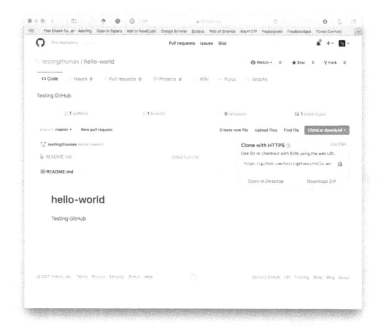

Figure 15: Cloning a repository.

previous changes included—and that this copy is connected to the repository on GitHub so we can push changes we make back up to GitHub.

So, if you have GitHub Desktop installed, click Open in Desktop. This should open the GitHub Desktop application, and the tool will ask you where to put your clone of the repository. You can put it wherever you like.

Once you have cloned the repository, you can see it in GitHub Desktop, including the history of previous changes. If you

Figure 16: Cloning your repository in GitHub Desktop.

just made the repository, as we did in the last chapter, you should have a single change, which contains the autogenerated README file. On the left of the application, you can see the repositories you have cloned on your computer. These do not necessarily have to be connected to GitHub, but if you have cloned them from there, they will be shown under the heading GitHub.

If you do not have GitHub Desktop installed—for example, if you are using git on a Linux machine—you can clone the repository on the command line. Here you need the URL you got by clicking the green button, and you need to run the command "git clone" like this:

Figure 17: See your repository in GitHub Desktop.

```
$ git clone \\
    https://github.com/testingthomas/hello-world.git
```

Modifying your local copy

Once you have cloned the repository, you can go to the directory where you put it. There, you can see the current version
of the code. If you just made the repository with a single
README file, that is all you will see. There is actually more
there; it is just hidden. You have a complete copy of the
repository, all previous revisions included. Git is a distributed
version control system, and you can interact with your local
clone for all your changes. If you don't want to, you do not

26

ever have to communicate with the remote repository that you cloned it from. Of course, if you don't, then others can't get to your changes—they can only see the public repository you have on GitHub—so eventually you do want to move changes back to GitHub. While you are actually working on your code, however, you will probably only interact with the copy.

As long as you only interact with the copy, you don't have to be online, so you can efficiently commit changes, switch branches (we cover branches in the next section), compare your current version with previous versions, etc. even if your Internet connection is very slow. Everything is kept on your own machine until you explicitly choose to interact with the GitHub copy.

How you create and change files is not affected by git. You can, for example, try to change the README file by adding a little description to it.

If you open GitHub Desktop after you have modified a file, you can see that you have Uncommitted Changes and if you pick the README.md file in the list of changes you can see what those changes are. Lines that have been deleted are shown in red and lines that have been added in green.

On the command line, you can get a list of modified files using:

```
$ git status
```

You can see the changes by using:

```
$ git diff
```

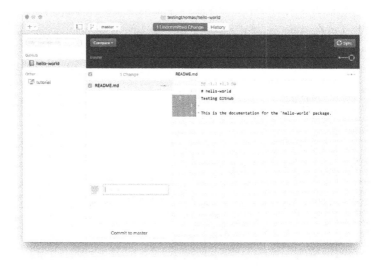

Figure 18: Modifications to your repository.

In GitHub Desktop there is no difference between files you have modified or new files you have created. With "git diff" they will be shown differently. You will treat them the same when you want to commit changes, though.

Staging, committing and pushing

When you have made changes to the repository, and you want to push those back to GitHub, you need to go through three steps—although the first two are somewhat merged in GitHub Desktop. The steps are staging changes, committing them, and pushing them upstream to the GitHub repository you cloned from.

28

Figure 19: Staging changes.

In GitHub Desktop you can see the modified files and what the changes are in the Uncommitted Changes tab. There are check buttons you can tick to select which files you want to commit to your repository. This is useful if you have changed several files but only want to commit some of your changes, but in general, branches are better for separating different sets of changes, so usually you want to commit all or nothing. They will all be ticked by default. Ticking the files here is called staging them. When you commit, only changes in staged files will be committed.

If you are interacting with git on the command line you can get the list of modified files using "git status", and you have to stage files explicitly. You do that with the command "git

29

Figure 20: Committing changes.

add". The "add" here doesn't just mean adding new files. You also add them if you want to commit files that you have changed. If you have changed README.md, then you write:

```
$ git add README.md
```

To commit your changes, you have to write a commit message. In GitHub Desktop you can give the commit a title and a description.

On the command line, you commit staged files with he command "git commit". This will open an editor where you can write the commit message. The first line in this message will be the title of the commit message and the rest the main message. You can also, if the message is short, use the option "-m":

```
git commit -m 'Added documentation to README.md'
```

Once you have committed the changes, GitHub Desktop will no longer show them as Uncommitted, of course, and neither will "git status". The "timeline" under the Sync button will indicate that you are ahead of the repository on GitHub, though. The last version you synchronised with is shown in a blue colour, and your current version is shown in grey to the right of it. If you make several commits, you will see a grey timeline stretching further and further to the right of the blue circle. Running "git status" will just tell you how many commits you are ahead of "origin/master" which is the "master" branch on the "origin" repository—the repository you have on GitHub.

To get your changes to go to the GitHub repository you have to push them. In GitHub Desktop you do not distinguish between pushing to the origin repository and pulling changes from it; you have a single button, Sync, that does both. Press it, and your local changes will be pushed to GitHub.

On the command line, you have to run the command:

```
$ git push
```

Fetching and pulling

The "origin" repository can also be ahead of your local clone. This can happen if you have allowed others to push changes

Figure 21: Committed changes.

to it, or if you have pushed changes from another clone of the repository, for example from another computer.

If this is the case, git will not allow you to push changes upstream. You first have to pull the upstream changes downstream to your own clone before you can push your local changes upstream. There are also two commands involved in this step, but GitHub Desktop wraps them both up in the Sync button. On the command line, you can get information about which changes have occurred upstream using the "git fetch" command—this will synchronise your local repository, so you get all the information available on the upstream repository, but it will not update your current version of the code, merely make it available to you. You can pull

32

the changes downstream and synchronise your code with the current version on the upstream repository using the "git pull" command.

When you pull changes downstream, git will merge them with your own changes. Most of the time, this will cause no problems because the changes are in different files or at least at different places of the same files. But, it happens that you have made changes at the same location both in your local clone and the upstream repository. If this happens, you have a conflict. If you have a conflict, git will still merge the changes, but it will mark the files with conflicts, so you know you have to deal with them. They will be shown as modified, and both versions of changes will be shown in the files. Typically in the format:

```
<<<<<<<
Your local changes
=======
The upstream changes
>>>>>>>
```

However, this can vary depending on how git is set up.

The easiest way to resolve the conflict is to go in and pick the version you want, or possibly make a compromise between the two.

Once you have resolved the conflict, you stage the fixed files. You can then commit them and push them upstream (or Sync them in GitHub Desktop).

Chapter 5

Branching and merging

If you work on a project on your own, and if you always stick to doing one thing at a time, you don't really need to use branches. If you work with others, or if you tend to work on more than one feature at a time, branches are the mechanism you need to keep separate sub-projects isolated from each other until they are ready to be merged into the main code base. The operations for working with branches are fast operations in git, so there is virtually no overhead in using them.

Creating and switching to a branch

When you want to develop a new feature, you first want to create a branch to develop it on, unless the new feature is trivial to implement. Then the changes can be handled in a single commit to the master branch without the risk of the changes interfering with anything else.

Figure 22: Creating a new branch.

In GitHub Desktop you can create a new branch from the toolbar. You have to click the icon that looks like a fork in a road, next to the drop-down that says master. The name master refers to the default branch that you are on initially; you can switch between branches using this dropdown button.

When you click on the button for creating new branches, you can give the new branch a name. You can try making the branch "new-feature" in your "hello-world" repository.

After you have created the new branch, you are automatically moved to that branch. You can see that you are on the new branch because the master button now says new-feature.

On the timeline below the toolbar, you can also see that you

Figure 23: Naming the branch.

are on the branch new-feature that has branched off master.

Try making some changes to the repository in the new branch. You can, for example, create three new files:

```
touch foo bar baz
```

Commit these changes, and you will see that your current point on the timeline moves along the new-feature branch and not the master branch. New changes, e.g.

```
echo foo >> foo
echo bar >> bar
echo baz >> baz
```

37

Figure 24: Working on the new branch.

modifies the local repository, as we would expect, and committing it updates the new-feature branch.

The Sync button is gone and is replaced by a Publish button. This is because the origin repository does not yet know about the new branch. If you Publish the branch, you get the Sync button back. Synchronising now, though, updates the new-feature branch. If you look at the repository on GitHub, you won't see the changes you just made on the main page.

You should, however, see a yellow box above the code that highlights that you have just pushed a new branch onto the repository. There is a green button in that box that says Compare & pull request.

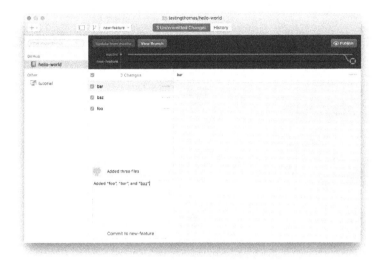

Figure 25: Branch with new files.

Making a pull-request from a branch

If you click the Compare & pull request button, you get sent
to a page for opening a new pull-request. Pull-requests are
the mechanism you generally use to communicate changes
to repositories you are not controlling yourself. You are
requesting the owner of a repository to pull your changes,
rather than pushing the changes yourself—in repositories you
do not own you might not have permission to push changes,
but the owner will have authority to pull them from you into
the repository. Thus the name.

When you open a pull request, you should give it a name and
describe which changes you have made on the branch you

Figure 26: Branch with modifications.

are asking to be pulled. This description can be written in Markdown with GitHub extensions that let you refer to other developers, repository issues, or other pull-requests.

Once you have described the pull-request, you can create it. This creates a page with the description you made and a list of the changes that you've done to the branch. If the pull-request can be merged without conflicts, there will be a green button for that. If there are conflicts, you will need to resolve those before the pull request can be merged.

Generally, these pull requests can also be used for discussions about the changes. You can add comments to pull requests, and you can review the changes to the code they will make.

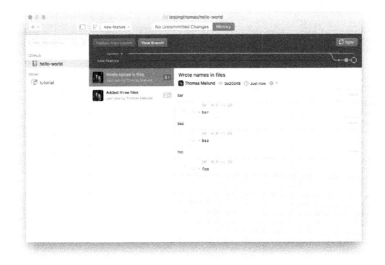

Figure 27: Synchronised branch.

This makes them useful for collaborations even when you do have permission to merge branches direction. If several developers are working on a project, pull requests give everyone a chance to review changes before they make it into the master branch.

If you are ready to merge the pull request, you can click the Merge pull request button. After that, you can add a small message to the merge.

After merging you can delete the branch that you used to implement the feature.

Back in your clone, you are still on the "new-feature" branch, even if you deleted it when merging the pull request. The

Figure 28: Pull request button on GitHub.

branch is still there in your clone, and you are still on it.

You can select the "new-feature" pull-down button and switch to the "master" branch.

On the "master" branch you will see that the last change was a merge with the pull-request you made.

Merging a branch

If you are the only developer on a project, merging new features into the "master" branch through pull requests is a bit cumbersome. It is still a good idea to implement new

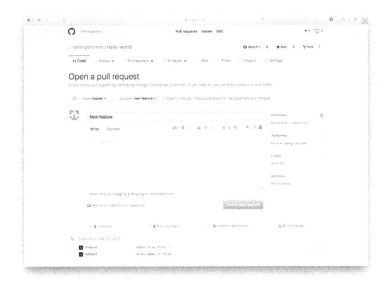

Figure 29: Creating a pull request.

features on separate branches, but you probably want to merge them into "master" when you are done with the features— there is no need to go through a review process if you wrote the code yourself and you are the only one to review it.

You can easily merge branches without pull requests, though. Try making a new branch, "new-feature-2", say, and make some changes to it, e.g. delete the "foo", "bar", and "bar" files we added in the "new-feature" pull-request.

Commit those changes to the branch.

Now, pick the branch selection button and switch to the "master" branch.

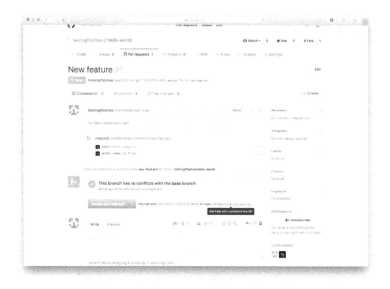

Figure 30: Describing the pull request.

On the "master" branch you shouldn't see the changes you made on branch "new-feature-2", but you can merge them into the branch. To do that, you need to pick the main menu item Branch > merge into "master".[1]

You then pick the branch to merge—in this case, "new-feature-2".

The result is the same as if you had used a pull request. The "master" branch now has the changes you made on the feature branch and the last change in the history is the merge.

---

[1]The menu item might be called merge into current branch or use a different name than "master", depending on which branch you are on.

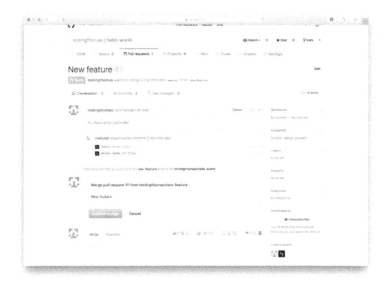

Figure 31: Merging the pull request, i.e. merging the two branches.

From the website, you can also inspect different branches from a pull-down button in the Code tab.

Just above this pull-down button is a box where you can access commits, branches, releases, and contributors. If you pick branches here, you can get to a page where you can control branches. You can delete branches you no longer need here.

If you pick the tab Graphs and then Network you will get a visualisation of the various branches in the repository's history and how they connect. For complex histories, this can be quite helpful.

Figure 32: Merged pull request page.

Branches on the command line

You can, of course, also manage branches on the command line. To create and switch to a branch, "new-feature", you use the "git checkout" command:

```
$ git checkout -b new-feature
```

To switch back to the "master" branch, you also use "git checkout" but leave out the "-b":

```
$ git checkout master
```

Figure 33: Back to GitHub Desktop.

Generally, you switch between existing branches with "checkout" and create new ones with "checkout -b".

If you want the new branch to exist in the origin repository on GitHub as well as in your clone, you can push it there with

```
$ git push origin new-feature
```

After that, you can make a pull-request as described above.

To merge a branch into "master", switch to master and run the "git merge" command:

```
git checkout master
```

Figure 34: Changing branch.

```
git merge new-feature
```

To delete the branch, run this:

```
git branch -D new-feature
```

To get a list of the existing branches, you write:

```
git branch
```

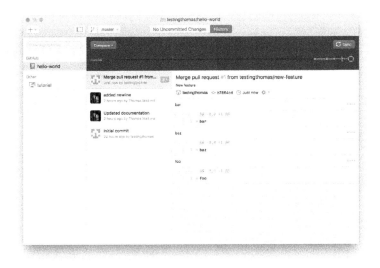

Figure 35: Back at the master branch.

GitFlow and other workflows using branches

There are several ways you can use branches in your development. See Atlassian's tutorial for a list of different options. One widespread use of branches is known as GitFlow. Here you have two main branches, "master" where you put stable versions of your software and "develop" where you have development code. When you want to create a new feature, you branch off from "develop" and implement it on a separate branch, and when you are done you merge it back into "develop". Bugfixes you branch of "master", fix the bugs, then merge the branch back into "master" but also "develop" so the bugs get fixed both places. When making new releases,

49

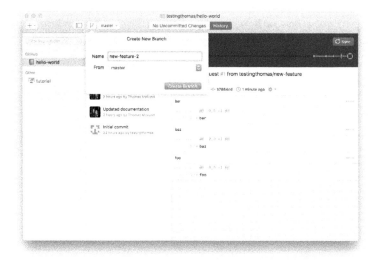

Figure 36: Creating yet another new branch.

you merge the "develop" branch into "master".

This is a very robust design of branches but can be a little over-kill for smaller projects. It is a good idea always to implement new features on separate branches, though, and if you plan to make pull-requests to other people's repositories, you definitely want to do that from different branches.

Figure 37: Modifying the branch.

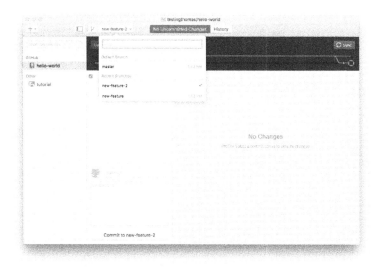

Figure 38: Back to master.

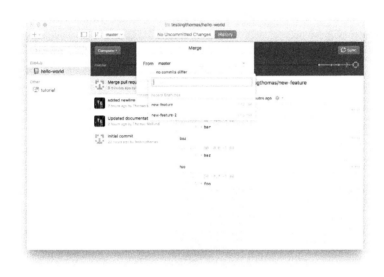

Figure 39: Merging into the master branch in GitHub Desktop.

Figure 40: Selecting the branch to merge.

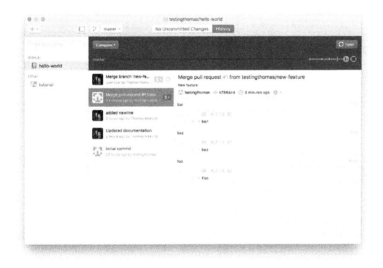

Figure 41: The master branch after the merge.

Figure 42: Selecting branches on the GitHub webpage.

Figure 43: Branch overview on the GitHub website.

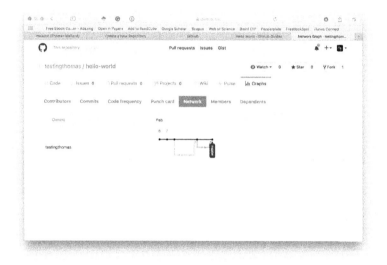

Figure 44: Graph view of branches and merges.

Chapter 6

Collaboration

If you only use repositories for projects to work on alone, you don't really need GitHub. You can just set up git on your on your own machine. There is, of course, some benefits it having the repository on a remote server, backups for example, but you don't need to push changes to the origin unless you plan for the people to see them. Where having a web interface to your repository is a significant benefit, is in collaborations with others.

There are two ways that you can collaborate on making changes to a repository: you can have a group of people that all have write-access to the repository so they all can push changes and merge pull-requests, or you can move changes from one repository to another through pull-requests. The former requires that you explicitly configure the repository so that all collaborators have write-access, the latter requires no setup at all, but does put the responsibility of merging pull-requests on the maintainer of a repository.

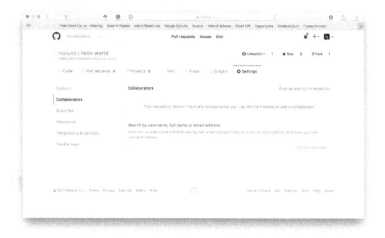

Figure 45: Collaborators section.

Collaborators on a project

If you have a group of people, who are collaborating on a project, you can set up the repository such that everyone has write access. To do that, you have to go to the Settings tab and then select Collaborators in the menu on the left.

You can then search for the people you want to add, by name, email address, or GitHub user-name and then add them.

They will then receive an invitation email. Following the link, there will send them to a webpage where they can accept the invitation. After that, your new collaborators can push to the repository.

If you set up a repository so several people can all push to it, you, of course, increase the risk that your changes can

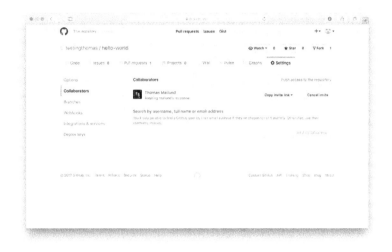

Figure 46: Finding collaborators.

interfere with each other. So, although it isn't necessary to use separate branches and pull-requests to collaborate in this scenario, it is an excellent idea to still do this.

Working on separate branches ensures that you will not commit changes to the main branch that can leave the repository in a state where the code doesn't work, irritating your fellow developers. Keeping your development on separate branches until they are ready to be merged into the master branch minimises the conflicts between different changes. Merging changes into the master branch via pull requests gives everyone a chance to see what is about to be merged and is an excellent opportunity for code review and discussion.

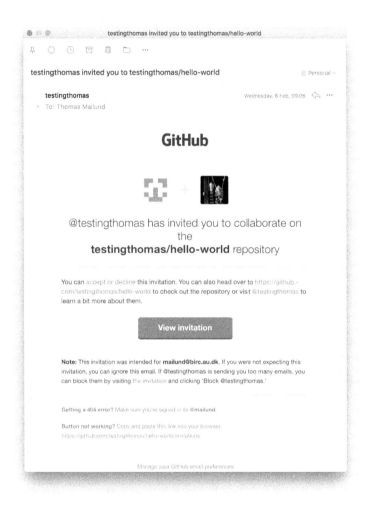

Figure 47: Collaboration invitation.

Figure 48: Accepting the collaboration invitation.

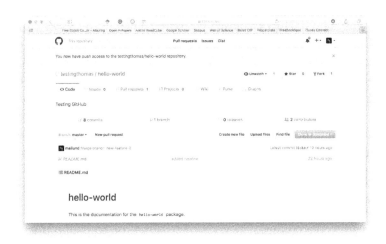

Figure 49: Push access to a repository.

Forking repositories

To collaborate on a repository without first setting up collaborations, you can use GitHub's "fork" mechanism. If you take a repository that already exists on GitHub, you can make a "fork" of it. A fork is similar to a clone but is used as an "origin" repository for your interaction with GitHub. It will work as the repository you push your local changes to, but it remembers that it is a clone of another repository and you can use this to move changes further upstream through pull requests.

To make a fork you go to the repository you are interested in and click the Fork button in the upper right corner.

This makes a copy in your own space of repositories, and you can then clone this to your computer.

If you use GitHub Desktop you will see that the local clone looks very similar to a clone of your own repositories, but you have an extra button, Pull Request, in the upper right corner. This button connects your clone to the original repository. You can still make pull requests to your own, forked, repository—as described earlier—but this button gives you a convenient way of making pull requests to the repository you do not have push access to.

You can change your local clone and commit the changes, as you can with your own repositories.

If you make changes to your own clone, or someone pushes changes to the repository you forked, the timeline at the top of GitHub Desktop will show you as having branched off the original repository. If the changes are to the repository you

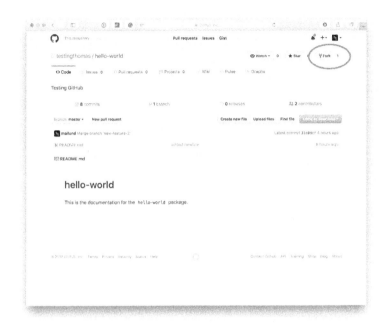

Figure 50: Forking a repository.

forked, you can merge those changes into your own clone by pressing the Update from... button.

If you interact with git on the command line, you can use

```
$ git remote
```

This will show you a list of the upstream repositories your clone knows about. If you have just forked a repository and done nothing else to modify the remote repositories you should

65

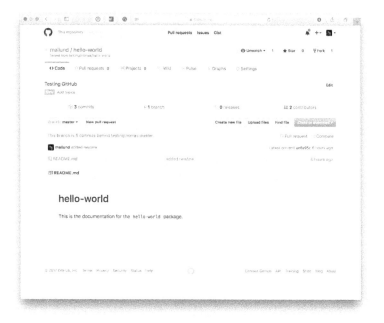

Figure 51: Webpage for a forked repository.

have one repository called "origin" and one that is named after the repository you forked. The "origin" repository is the default repository you will push to and pull from; the other you can only pull from unless you have been given write permission to it. To get synchronise from it, you use "fetch" and "pull" as you would from your "origin" clone of it, you have to add the name of it to the command.

For my copy of "hello-world", the forked repository is called "testingthomas":

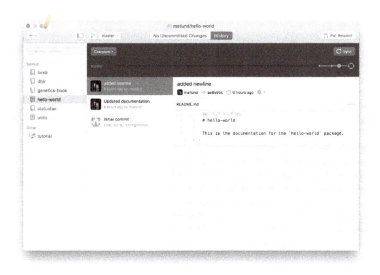

Figure 52: A forked repository in GitHub Desktop.

```
$ git remote
origin
testingthomas
```

I can fetch information about changes on it as

```
$ git fetch testingthomas
remote: Counting objects: 3, done.
remote: Compressing objects: 100% (2/2), done.
remote: Total 3 (delta 0), reused 3 (delta 0), pack-reused 0
Unpacking objects: 100% (3/3), done.
From https://github.com/testingthomas/hello-world
   e8f2cc2..83b71f0  master      -> testingthomas/master
```

Figure 53: Making changes to a forked repository.

and I can pull from it with

```
$ git pull testingthomas master
```

The second argument to the "pull" command is the branch you want to pull changes from. This argument is necessary when you pull from a repository that is not the default, i.e. "origin".

If you have made changes to your clone, you can start a pull request from GitHub Desktop by pressing the Pull Request button. You need to synchronise them to your "origin" repository—by pressing the Sync button—before you can do that. After you have done this, you can set up the pull request

Figure 54: Pulling updates from the original repository.

from inside the tool. You do not need to go to the GitHub webpage to do it.

You write the description for the pull request and press Send Pull Request. It will then appear as a pull request on the GitHub page for the original repository you forked from.

If you do not use GitHub Desktop, the easiest way to make a pull request is to go to your repository webpage. There, you have a New pull request button next to the branch pull-down button.

If you click it, you will be sent to a page that shows you the difference between the branch you want to merge from, in the forked repository, and the branch you want to merge into, in

69

Figure 55: Creating a pull request from GitHub Desktop.

the original repository. On this page, you can create a pull request by clicking the—not surprisingly—Create pull request button.

You really want to make a branch to use in pull requests, though. From the point that you make a pull request and until it is closed—either because it is rejected or merged. All changes that you make to the branch from which you made the pull request will also be included as updates to the pull request. So, if you make a pull request from your master branch, then all future changes you make to "master" will also be part of the pull request. You probably don't want that, so make sure you always make a branch for pull requests. You can choose which branch to use for a pull request from

70

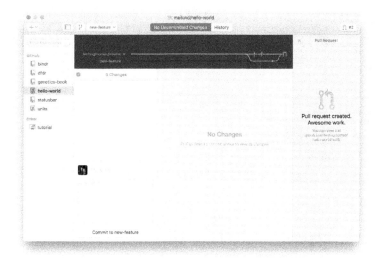

Figure 56: After the pull request.

the webpage.

Other than that, pull requests work the same between repositories as they do between branches in the same repository.

Issues and Projects

Two other GitHub features are worth mentioning when we discuss collaboration: Issues and Projects. The former is a bug- and feature-tracker, where people can add bug reports or feature requests and these can be discussed; the latter is a forum for planning and arranging ideas.

You should have an Issues tab on your repository webpage. If

71

Figure 57: A pull request from the forked repository.

you work on a forked repository it is best to put issues there, unless you have good reasons to keep them for yourself.

To create a new issue, you click the New issue button. You can then give the issue a title and write a description of it before submitting it.

When you have created an issue, you can discuss it by adding comments.

Each issue is given a number, shown next to the title. You

Figure 58: Create the pull request in the original repository.

can use this number to make cross-references between issues. If you write #3 in a comment somewhere, you will insert a link to issue number 3 and get a link from the issue back to the comment. If in a commit, you write "Resolves #3" or "Fixes #3" or something similar, you will automatically close the issue. If in a pull request, you mention an issue number, you will connect the issue and the pull request.

Projects are found under the Projects tab.

Figure 59: Choosing a branch for a pull request.

You don't have any in a new repository, but you can create as many as you want. To create one, you have to give it a title and optionally a description.

A new project doesn't look like much. It is just a place where you can create "columns", and when you do, you can create items in them.

These are just notes you can move between different topics, represented as the columns. GitHub projects are very similar

74

Figure 60: The issue page on GitHub.

to Trello boards in that regard but integrated with your repository.

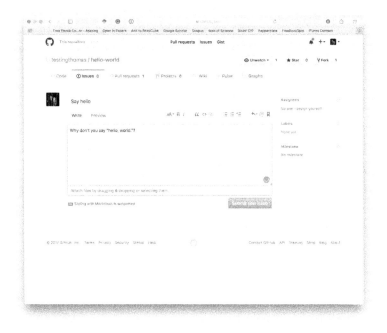

Figure 61: Creating an issue.

Figure 62: Discussing an issue.

Figure 63: The project page for your repository.

Figure 64: Creating a project.

Figure 65: An empty project.

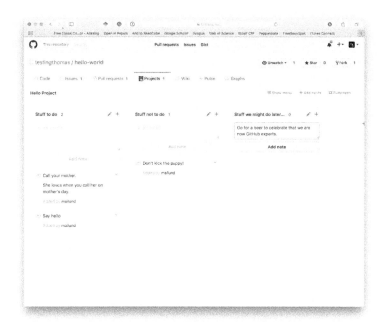

Figure 66: A project with items.

Chapter 7

Ecosystem of tools for ensuring high code quality

GitHub integrates with many online tools that you can use to test and analyse the quality of your code. Covering all the tools that integrate with GitHub is beyond this short book—you can find a complete list at the GitHub Integration Directory—but I will give you an overview that should give you an idea of what you can achieve by integrating code quality services with your repository.

Continuous integration with Travis

The term continuous integration refers to integration testing at regular intervals rather than only at the end of a project when you are combing all the components of your software. In

Figure 67: Signing into Travis.

the context we will use it here, you can think of it as running regular tests.

Through service integration, you have several choices for setting up continuous integration/testing in your GitHub repositories. These services are configured such that they run a suite of consistency checks and software tests each time you commit and/or each time someone makes a pull request.

One of the most popular of these services is Travis. To set up Travis for a repository, go to the Travis website and sign in using your GitHub account. Just click the button on the upper right of their webpage.

When you get in, you will get to a page that shows the recent

84

Figure 68: Recent tests.

tests of your repositories. Mine is shown below, but yours will be empty if it is the first time you log in.

You can click on My Repositories, though, and get a list of the repositories you have on GitHub. In this list, you can enable Travis.

As an example, I will set up testing for the repository mailund/searching. I enable that repository.

That, in itself, doesn't actually do anything.

Travis won't do anything until you push changes to the repository, and you need to add a Travis configuration file before that works. This file, a YAML file with the name .travis.yml, describes how your code should be built and how it should be

Figure 69: Adding a repository to Travis.

tested. How this file should look depends on the programming language you use in your repository. They all have different ways of building programs and running tests. You can read the Getting Started documentation to get an overview.

The repository I will be testing contains a simple C program. I use `make` to build the program, and I have set it up such that running `make test` will run tests. My `.travis.yml` file looks like this:

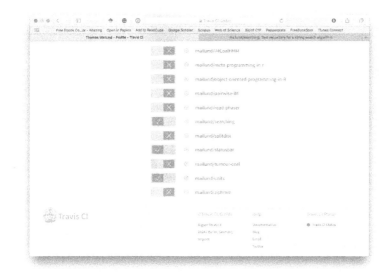

Figure 70: Enabling a repository.

```
language: c
script:
  - make
  - make test
```

The first line specifies that I am using the C programming
language and the **script** lines build the program and run the
tests.

If I push this file to GitHub, Travis will be informed of the
push and run a test. If you look at your commit log, you can
see that Travis is running. This is shown as a yellow dot next
to the commit.

87

Figure 71: An empty test page.

If you click on the dot, you will be sent to Travis where you can inspect the build and tests.

You don't have to sit and wait while Travis is testing your code—you will receive an email when it is done, telling you how the tests went.

Quite often, it takes me a few tries to get the testing environment set up correctly. Travis runs tests on a Linux machine by default, but you can set it up to test on other architectures and different environments. So because the environments are different, the tests sometimes fail even though they work on my computer. You can see failed attempts at getting Travis up and running—or just failed tests, which is of course also a

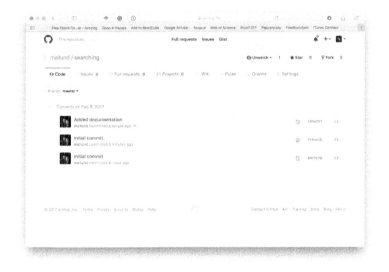

Figure 72: The commit log shows a running test.

possibility—in the commit log as red crosses.

Eventually, I get it right, and I get a green tick-mark next to the commit.

Code coverage

It is better to pass your tests than failing them, of course, but how much passing them says about your software depends on how exhaustive they are. If you only test a small percentage of your code, then passing every test does not say much about the majority of the code; what you don't test, they cannot inform you about.

89

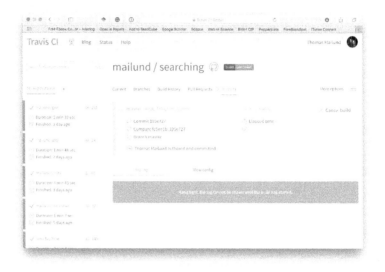

Figure 73: A test currently running on Travis.

You can set up tools to check how much of your code is actually tested when you run your test suite. Statistics about that is called code coverage statistics, and you can add that to your continuous integration setup.

Several services will check the code coverage of your repositories. One of them is Codecov. You can go there and sign in with your GitHub account.

When you do, you get a list of repositories it is checking for you. I have a few there, but if you just signed up, you will not have any yet.

You cannot enable code coverage testing directly from the webpage. Codecov needs to get code coverage statistics from

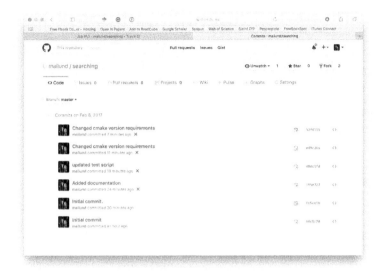

Figure 74: Failed tests.

your continuous integration test suite—it cannot figure out how to get it itself—so it will be waiting to receive these statistics before it displays any summary of it.

How code coverage is checked depends on the programming language as well. You can get a list of supported languages in the Codecov documentation. Most modern languages have great frameworks for pulling out code coverage statistics from running a test suite without modifying the tests. Unfortunately, C, the language I have chosen for the search tool, does not. Here, I need to compile the code with coverage flags—I can read in the Codecov documentation that if I use the `clang` compiler, I need to add the option `-coverage`—and I then

91

Figure 75: The most recent test passed.

need to use the `gcov` tool after running the tests.

I can set up the compiler flag in my `Makefile`. It now looks like this:

```
all: search

search: search.c
    cc -coverage search.c -o search
```

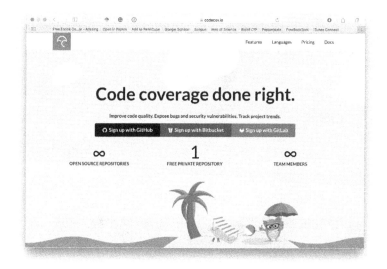

Figure 76: Signing into Codecov.

```
test: search test.sh
    ./test.sh
```

In the `.travis.yml` I need to set up that the compiler needs
to be **clang** and that the build should run **gcov search.c**
after running the tests. I also have to add a command for
sending the coverage statistics to Codecov. That command
should be put in the **after_success** field so it is only run
when all the tests are running—the instructions for what to
put I can get directly from the Codecov documentation.

```
language: c
script:
```

93

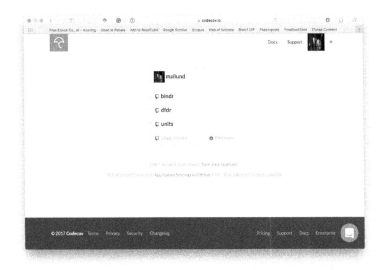

Figure 77: Repositories connect to Codecov.

```
    - make
    - make test
    - gcov search.c
compiler:
    - clang
after_success:
    - bash <(curl -s https://codecov.io/bash)
```

I now have to push these changes to GitHub. That will make
Travis build the tool and run the tests, and since the tests are
passing it will upload the statistics to Codecov. After it has
done that, the repository appears in the list of repositories
there.

Figure 78: Your repository has been added to Codecov.

If I then click on the repository name, I go to a dashboard showing the coverage statistics.

In this dashboard, you can see which parts of your code are not being tested if any, and after more than one commit you can also see a history of how coverage changes over time.

Ideally, you want your code coverage to be at 100%, or as near as you can get, at all time. Be careful, though. Even at 100%, you are only guaranteed that each statement in your code is executed in at least one test. It does not ensure that you are testing your code exhaustively. If you call a function somewhere in your code with a single test value, that

Figure 79: Coverage details on Codecov.

96

statement is marked as checked. It is possible that any other value you would give the function call would result in an error. Code coverage statistics only tell you about which parts of your code are tested and which are not; they cannot inform you about how appropriate your tests are. You still have to apply some critical thinking to writing useful tests. Code coverage is a great help, though, in making sure that you do not forget to test something.

It might look at little complicated to set up code coverage checking, but setting it up for my C program is a worst-case scenario. In many cases, you only need to add a few lines to the .travis.yml file. For example, to compute code coverage for an R package, you need to add these two lines and otherwise leave the code alone:

```
r_github_packages:
  - jimhester/covr
after_success:
  - Rscript -e 'covr::codecov()'
```

In Python projects, you can get away with adding this:

```
after_success:
  - coveralls
  - coverage xml
```

You can check the Codecov documentation for the language of your choice.

Automatic code review

There are tools for automatically testing the quality of your code. These look for various cases of potentially incorrect usage—accessing variables that are not guaranteed to be initialised, code that is never executed, etc.—and highlight these for you. You can make such an automated code review part of your continuous integration checking as well.

One such service is Codacy. You can go to Codacy and sign up with your GitHub account.

Once you have signed in, you get a list of the repositories you have set up there. I have the two listed below; you will not have any yet.

You can click the Add project button to set one up.

That sends you to a list of repositories, and you can select which to add to Codacy. I will add my search program.

This starts a code review; it is a slow process, so you have to wait for a little before you get any results back.

You will get an email when it is done. You can then go back to Codacy and see a report of what it has found. If you are lucky, it found no issues. If not, you have a list of items you can check out and try to resolve.

If you want to set up Codacy, so it runs a code review each time you push to your repository, you can set that up in Settings > Integration. You need to enable the Post-Commit Hook. Instructions there will guide you through the setup process. You probably want this, so you don't have to ask for reviews from time to time manually.

Figure 80: Signing up to Codacy.

Figure 81: Project status on Codacy.

Figure 82: Connecting a new project (i.e. repository).

Figure 83: Your new project is under review.

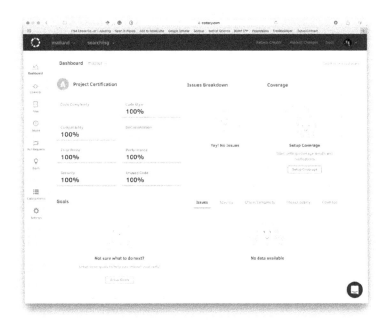

Figure 84: Details of a review.

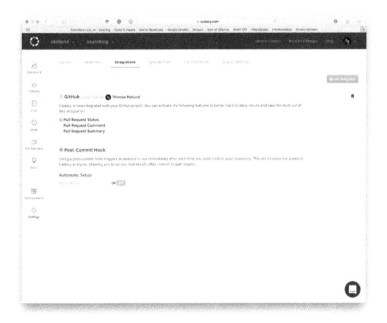

Figure 85: Connect GitHub to Codacy, so it shows you the
status of each commit.

Chapter **8**

Conclusions

You have now seen the primary use of git and GitHub, the use patterns that will cover 99% of your interaction with GitHub. You have seen how you can create and interact with your own repositories, how you can fork other repositories and send pull requests to them, and how you can integrate your repositories with the ecosystem of code quality and testing tools integrated with GitHub.

There is, of course, more you can do with GitHub than what I have covered in this short book. I haven't told you how move an existing project to GitHub, or how you can migrate from another version control system, but I trust you now know enough of git and GitHub that you will be able to figure such issues out yourself if you need to. You can start at the git documentation webpage.

From here on forward, to get familiar with GitHub, you need to use it from day to day. It will soon become second nature for you to commit and push your changes to git, and if you get involved in collaboration projects, you will soon get familiar with the use of pull requests for adding and discussing new features. You know enough to get started, so go and get more experience!

If you liked this book, please drop me a line, write a review on Goodreads or Amazon, check out my other books, or sign up to my mailing list to be informed of new books. And if you find something interesting in my own repositories on GitHub do feel free to send me a pull request. I look forward to hearing from you.

www.ingramcontent.com/pod-product-compliance
Lightning Source LLC
Chambersburg PA
CBHW071257050326
40690CB00011B/2434